Uneventful Reminiscences

This catalogue has been published on the occassion of
an exhibition organized by Hollis Taggart Galleries
presented from 28 November 2000 to 13 January 2001.

Provenance and further details can be provided by the gallery upon request.
All works described as "estate stamped" bear the name "F. C. Frieseke."

ISBN: 0-9705723-0-1
Library of Congress Card Catalogue Number: 00-109672

Cover: *Canoeing, Florida*, (detail), 1921. Page 47
Endpages: *Fishing, Florida* (detail), c. 1921. Page 30

Hollis Taggart Galleries
48 East 73 Street, New York, NY 10021
Tel 212 628 4000 Fax 212 717 4119
www.HollisTaggart.com

Publication Coordination: Connie Freeman and Kirsten Olds
Design: Russell Hassell, New York
Printing: Capital Offset, Concord, New Hampshire
Photography: Helga Photo Studio, New York

Uneventful Reminiscences

A Childhood in Florida   FREDERICK C. FRIESEKE

Hollis Taggart Galleries   48 East 73 Street   New York City 10021

I N 1881, AFTER THE DEATH OF HIS MOTHER, seven-year-old Frederick Frieseke and his older sister, Edith, were taken by their father to Jacksonville, Florida. They remained for four years, during which time their father, Herman Frieseke, established a brick-making operation. Frederick never returned, and lived all his adult life in France. But this journey—the four-year stay at an impressionable age in Florida, with its exotic inhabitants and landscapes—were to be touchstones for my grandfather's imagination, even to the point of homesick nostalgia, for the rest of his life.

The watercolors that illustrate this memoir were painted in 1921. As a young man, Frieseke had gone to Paris to study painting. Though he showed his work regularly in the United States, his career remained focused in France—in Paris, Giverny, and finally in Normandy, where he died in 1939. He married Sarah O'Bryan in 1905. The couple had one child, a daughter (my mother Frances), who was born in Paris in 1914.

Frieseke's career as a painter enjoyed considerable success in the second decade of the 1900s, when he was best known for impressionistic renditions of women in flowering gardens, and for interior scenes of women in their boudoirs. Examples of his work can be found in the collections of most major art museums in the United States.

Around 1920, his career well established, Frieseke encountered, in a lecture by a critic (who may have been citing John Ruskin or William Hazlitt), the suggestion that a painting of landscape, even if done right on the spot, is still an exercise of memory. The artist must look away from the scene in order to see the canvas, and in so doing, must lose direct contact with the source of the image that inspires the painting. If this were true, Frieseke reasoned, perhaps the length of time between the visual experience of the landscape and its rendition in paint did not matter. As an experiment, he set out to recall scenes familiar from his childhood in Florida. Working in watercolor, he began to create the images that appear in this book. Later, he used many of these watercolors as the basis for an interesting series of oil paintings, which—despite the fact that they were of subjects for which he was not well known—he thought enough of to exhibit in Paris (at the Galeries Durand-Ruel in 1926 and the Salon des Tuilleries in 1927) and in New York (at the Brooklyn Museum of Art in 1927 and at the Macbeth Gallery in 1929).

How deeply Frieseke felt about his time in Florida is demonstrated in a letter Sadie (as Frieseke called her—he answered to her "Freddy") wrote to their daughter in January 1928, shortly after the series of paintings of Florida subjects had been finished. She and Frederick had gone to Nice, in the south of France, leaving Frances with a governess in Paris. "Yesterday at four o'clock we went to the casino to hear the Fisk Jubilee Singers, a sextet of Negroes. They sang so beautifully, all the things that Papa used to hear the workmen on his father's place sing, when he was a boy. It made him weep."

Six years later, in 1934, Frances, who had some ambitions to become a writer, wrote a memoir of her childhood in Giverny during the war, which she called *It's Only the Cannon*. She gave the book, which included illustrations supplied by Frieseke, to her mother as a present. Impressed by his daughter's efforts, Frieseke dictated his own boyhood memories to Frances, who jotted them down, probably while she was modeling for her father, since she often sat for his paintings. That memoir, to which Frieseke added marginal illustrations in pen and ink, provides the text for this volume, which he, with characteristic modesty, titled *Uneventful Reminiscences.*

What follows, both in words and images, is a charming document that recounts life on the Florida frontier in the 1880s: the side-wheelers and ruffians, crabs and orange groves, snakes and sunsets. It represents a time not long after the Civil War, and was meant only for the author's family's eyes. Bringing it to publication after the time that it describes, we cannot fail to notice the occasional jocular tone with which my grandfather (educated and fortunate as he was) spoke what may seem patronizingly (and generically) of the less fortunate or less educated (whether "Negro" or "cracker"). I am confident that Frieseke had no intention to offend anyone. Certainly his grandchildren, who offer this book for publication, intend no slight to anyone.

Although they lived in France, both Frederick and Sarah Frieseke were American-born, and neither would have considered surrendering American identity. Unlike many U. S. citizens, they had stayed in France during the First World War.

Nonetheless, now and then, as the world changed, and as Frances got older, they sometimes contemplated returning to America. After Frances was engaged to be married, and once it was clear that she would live in the United States, conversation on the subject of the Friesekes' return continued. In the spring of 1937, Frieseke wrote to his dealer, Robert Macbeth, "To be sure, at my age I had hoped my next change would be direct to Heaven but if needs must—curiously you speak of Florida and I have had Florida in my mind as the only place in America that would tempt me, though I should find it sadly changed since my boyhood there, overrun by trailers etc. However, the idea appeals strongly to me."[1]

With the announcement of Frances's pregnancy at the end of the year, the issue of the Friesekes' possible return took on additional impetus. On the eve of the outbreak of the Second World War, in August 1939, they were on the point of visiting Frances's family (her first son, Hugh, had been born the previous year) when Frieseke died suddenly. And so their speculation concerning a return remained only speculation. As Frieseke had written in 1934, "I like that country. It still enchants me."

The family hopes that, somewhat more than a century after he experienced that country, Frieseke's memories of it will enchant others as well.

—NICHOLAS KILMER

1. Letter from F. C. Frieseke to Robert Macbeth, April 22, 1937, Archives of American Art, Microfilm Collection, Macbeth Gallery Papers, frame NMc46.505

My MOTHER HAD DIED. A business opportunity called my father to Florida and he decided to take us with him: my sister Edith, a motherly little girl of ten, and myself, seven.

I remember little of the five-day voyage. I was train sick most of the time. Cincinnati stands out: dark night and a hill opposite the station sprinkled with lights like stars.

When the conductor passed my sister would nudge me. "Squeeze down, Freddy." She feared he would think me a big boy to be traveling half fare. I was quite small, really.

NIGHT, ORANGE GROVE, 1921. Watercolor on paper, 7¾ × 10¹⁄₁₆ inches. Signed lower right: "F. C. Frieseke"

Finally we entered the pinewoods of Georgia. The train stopped for some reason, I believed in order to let us pick flowers, yellow jasmine. My father had disappeared. As the train was slowly starting we were worried. My sister took me by the hand. "Come, Freddy," she said. Fortunately my father entered the car as we were leaving.

At one stop my father took us to see a cotton gin. Father spoke to the operator of the lever. The man pointed to a notice board. "Don't talk to the operator." I was embarrassed for my father but he did not seem unduly crushed.

The Spanish moss dripping from the live oaks and the
Negro villages in the pine clearings were strange to us.

We arrived at my Uncle Albert's one evening. We were
to spend the winter with his family. They lived on the Saint
John's river opposite Jacksonville.

He was a jeweler and a saint. There was also my Aunt Fannie
and three boy cousins, Karl, Albert and Harry. Karl, about my own
age, was so freckled that the real boy was almost invisible.
He had been able to "lick" me when they visited us in the north.
Now he couldn't and we got on very well.

following page: THE JETTY, 1921. Watercolor on paper, 7½ × 10 inches. Signed lower right: "F. C. Frieseke"

On our first night we children sat on the back porch in the moonlight and I fell off the steps and broke my arm. I am still inclined to break myself in spots.

My Aunt Fannie's parents lived in the orange grove next to ours. They had two fascinating grown sons. One, Alan, was a taxidermist. He kept tiny alligators in a tank and would stuff them. An alligator mounted on a bent tree trunk of papier maché and reflected in a poisonous looking green pool, was greatly in demand by the northern tourists, as were the Florida scenes by Ransom, always sunsets because the conch shells, on which they were painted, were a beautiful rose color.

preceding page: BLUE BOAT, SMALL FIGURES, PALMS, 1921. Watercolor on paper, 8⅛ × 10⅝ inches. Signed by the artist, reinforced with Estate stamp lower left

I admired them greatly and determined I should paint on
conch shells when I grew up. Or maybe I would stuff alligators.

My Uncle Albert, not very strong, liked working at his home
in the country and made breast pins and bangles of alligator teeth,
handsomely capped with gold.

I thought perhaps I'd like that better, after all.

Jonas was a hunchbacked Negro who worked for my uncle.
We would sit in his hut in the evenings and beg for stories.
He'd say, "What you want me to tell stories for? It's wicked.
I'll tell you a tale." And we liked that as well.

One night he was boiling molasses candy and at a dramatic point of his tale he tipped over the pot and we suffered a good deal even after he had scraped the candy (and skin) off our knees, legs and feet. But we did not complain too much till the tale was finished.

My aunt had a washerwoman, Winnie, whose son was a playmate of ours. Her husband was named Mosely, and was a giant. He worked for my father, helped pole a "lighter" or flatboat, when he wasn't preaching. He found preaching less fatiguing.

My father's business in the south was manufacturing bricks. Previously bricks came from the north. He brought with him white overseers. The workmen were all blacks.

WOMAN WITH BASKET ON HEAD, 1921. Watercolor on paper, 7½ × 9½ inches. Estate stamped lower right

That winter we attended a private school kept
by a charming southern lady whose husband, brave
fellow, was "resting," and had been, since the Civil War.
The school was some three miles up the river and we could
go either by road through the pinewoods, or in a rowboat, the latter
a bit hazardous for children as the river, in that section, was quite
five miles wide.

One day we were going by road and my sister was conducting
her small troop of four. We had passed, with some tremors, the house
of a nice old Irish couple, whose house, built something like a boat,

was reputed (by us) to be haunted. Still looking back over our shoulders, half hoping to see a small ghost, nothing important, we came to the Negro village, usually a point of great delight to us.

Today, however, there was a yellow rag hanging from a window. My sister said, "Quick, children, put your hands over your mouth and don't breathe 'till we get by. Smallpox."

We might have turned back, rather than run the terrible danger, but it didn't occur to my sister. We passed, arriving at the settlement limits, with purple faces and bursting lungs. Myself, I had blown up long ago, and had given myself up for lost.

We hastened on to the little "hammock," a depression, semi-tropical in foliage. At the foot of the steep path was a cold spring. We quickly made cups out of magnolia leaves, and took long antiseptic drinks.

On reaching school, our teacher told us that we had probably overestimated the danger, but complimented my sister just the same.

I think it was the same day that I fell from a limb, or at least fell as far as the broken stub of a branch, which had hooked in the seat of my small knickers, would let me. My sister, never strong at climbing trees, was up this one like a flash. I was unhooked, but unfortunately she had not allowed for the laws of gravitation.

HUNTING ALLIGATORS, 1921. Watercolor on paper, 7 ⁹⁄₁₆ × 10⅛ inches. Signed lower right: "F. C. Frieseke"

I wasn't much hurt. She covered me with her apron and hurried me back to the school and sewed me up.

I had to take very short steps going home. She had done a thorough job and sewed my pants legs together to the knees.

I complained a little, but she said, "Well, Freddy, I did all I could." And she had!

I was somewhat comforted at spying a handsome watermelon in the middle of the road. On picking it up, I was amazed at its having practically no weight. Some other child had made a small hole and scooped it empty. It had been an entirely unlucky day for me.

Once when my sister and I were leaving the wharf, after a trip to Jacksonville, we saw a group near the shore. As we approached, my sister said, "Don't look, Freddy." A drowned man had washed ashore. Always there has been someone to say to me, "Don't look, Freddy."

The brickyards were some miles from our home. My father often took me with him on his morning drive to the works.

It was a beautiful road: first through the pines, here and there a Negro hut, then a pond which I always eyed carefully, rarely disappointed in spying an alligator stretched on a log.

Shortly beyond was an abandoned plantation, the fine old colonial mansion half hidden by the live oaks and chinaberry trees.

The Negro quarters were sparsely occupied. To a nearby tree were still attached the rings to which the slaves were once tied for punishment. At the ruined entrance of the drive Aunt Julia, an ancient Negress, was often waiting for a little chat with my father, with tales of bad old days—and sometimes not so bad.

Further along the white sand road we would come to a hammock through which a clear stream flowed, and there were always flowers and gorgeous insects. Beyond was a cypress swamp, hideous and gloomy,

PLANTATION HOUSE (HOTEL JACKSONVILLE), 1921. Watercolor on paper, 7½ × 9½ inches. Estate stamped lower right

with the gaunt cypress knees swarming over the stagnant water, the home of alligators and water moccasins. Nothing could have tempted me near it. Soon singing would reach us, beautiful singing: a gang of Negroes naked to the waist, chopping wood to feed the furnaces. Beyond these we passed an ugly boarding house for the northern whites, and we were there.

Even a brickyard can be beautiful in that country. The lazing workmen would be momentarily electrified into movement by my father's arrival. Perhaps Mosely would be singing, improvising:

Look at the sun

He look so high

Then I got to work

'Cause the boss man's nigh.

Soon I go home

When the whistle blow

Then I'se out of a job

'Cause I'se so slow.

Then the boss man's son . . . etc. etc.

The engineer once showed me a rattlesnake over four feet long, which he had found coiled in the ashes that morning, and killed.

I would go down to the wharf on the little creek, through which the lighters were poled to the Saint John's River to be picked up by a tug and towed to Jacksonville.

This was a favorite spot of mine. While I quietly fished with a hand line I would keep my eyes open for any wild life in the jungle opposite. Once an otter swam the river. Moccasins and alligators were no longer a novelty. Sometimes a flamingo or a pelican crossed the narrow

FISHING, FLORIDA, c. 1921. Watercolor on paper, 9 × 12 inches. Signed lower right: "F. C. Frieseke." Private collection

opening in the treetops. Flaming cardinal redbirds flashed through the branches, and hummingbirds always. Deep in the clear water the fish, spotted fish, red fish, striped fish, black, blue, impossible fish.

I liked that country. It still enchants me, though I have never returned.

Sometimes, as I fished, a faint, high tenor gradually became more distinct and a lighter crept 'round the bend; Henry King and a comrade poling an empty flatboat back from Jacksonville, and Henry singing:

Knock at the door, and the door fly open

And the love it come a tinkling down.

That winter my father built a house. He had bought some land on the river and planted an orange grove. Houses were built on piles, with a clearance of about three feet, for coolness.

On rainy days we played under the house. The billows of white sand made a splendid sea on which to navigate our craft, usually steamboats made of hand-split cypress shingles, on which empty tomato cans were nailed. Quite good "steam" could be kept up with small pine knots. I had rather a good side-wheeler with a clockwork engine. I don't recall its ever working, and being a bit reactionary myself, I preferred sail. I took Webster's unabridged and

33

following page: FLORIDA STROLLERS, BOARDWALK, 1921. Watercolor on paper, 7½ × 9½ inches. Signed by the artist, reinforced with Estate stamp lower left

learned, by heart, the complete rigging of a full-rigged ship. I have not since found this knowledge of particular use to me.

I learned to swim at this time; learned through being pushed off the dock by larger boys.

I did some farming: grew peanuts, which the salamanders (or pocket gophers) ate; and pineapples, which refused to develop.

I also trapped. My father paid me ten cents for a salamander, five cents for rats, in moderation; twenty-five cents for 'possums and foxes.

Our nearest neighbors were Major B—and his wife. The major was

preceding page: VERANDA, SLEEPING DOG, 1921. Watercolor on paper, 7⅝ × 10¹/₁₆ inches. Signed by the artist, reinforced with Estate stamp lower right

pompous, convivial, an accomplished liar, and wholly delightful. Often he would knock on my window in the early morning, to take me fishing.

We would row up the river to where a cane-bordered creek flowed in, up this creek a mile or so, and anchor. Nothing was ever more lovely than the sunrise here, reflected in the still water. Flocks of white cranes flying overhead, an eagle high in the air, a fish hawk rising with its prey and the eagle dropping like a stone would catch the fish, wisely released by the hawk, before it touched the water.

The major was frequently sober at this hour. One day, not so early, his horse escaped him and ran playfully in circles. The major, red in the face from effort and libations, seeing me looking on, cried harshly, "Fred, the next time he passes you, just knock him down."

I wondered if my size would warrant this, and concluded not.

The major was useful in an emergency. I had a new knife and at once tested it on my finger. My sister and I were alone that day. She clutched me by the arm and rushed me over to the major, who was fortunately at home. Without a moment's hesitation he snatched a

FISHING IN THE SWAMP, 1921. Watercolor on paper, 7¾ × 9¾ inches. Signed lower left: "F. C. Frieseke"

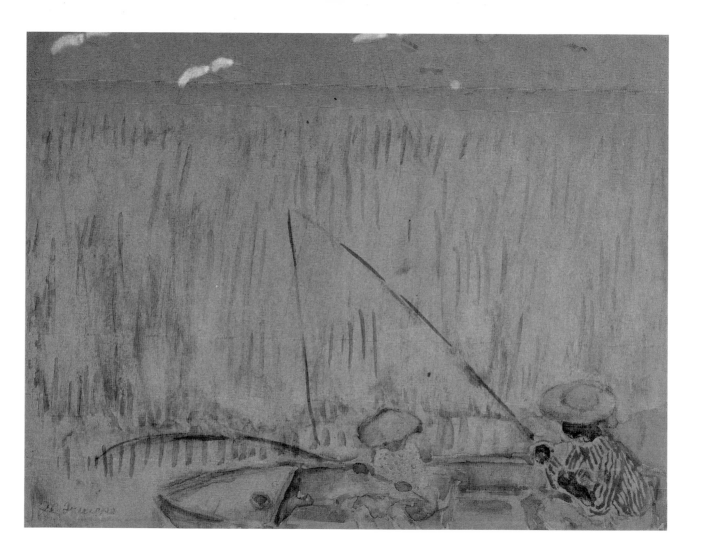

large chew of tobacco from his mouth and slapped it on the wound.

"There," he said.

I felt relief at once. The smart was so much worse than the original pain.

The major was particularly favored by the elements. A fence separated his orange grove from ours. If our oranges were frosted, his were not touched. If rain were not needed and we were flooded, none fell on his side of the fence. Of this he would assure you while you stood staring at his guttered and gullied garden.

His stories of his war experiences (I believe he had not once quit Baltimore during those sad years) thrilled us.

His wife treated us to what she called Baltimore biscuits. They would have made excellent grapeshot, should hostilities again have broken out.

Mrs. B—had a packing case full of old paper-backed novels, Seaside Library and others. I read them all. I recall the satisfactory ending of one. The pirate captain was bound to the tomb of his first wife, with arms outstretched pointing right and left to the headstones of

41

following page: FISHING FROM A JETTY, 1921. Watercolor on paper, 7½ × 9½ inches. Signed lower right: "F. C. Frieseke"

his second and third. There he was left for the tropical sun and the land crabs to execute justice, while the avengers, disgruntled lovers from the Middle West, sailed into the sunset.

My literary tastes thus formed now admit the modern detective story, provided lovers are kept in the background and no stupidities such as suicides and homicidal maniacs be allowed.

I wish my criminals to be fully cognizant of their iniquities, and to be treated as such.

Major and Mrs. B—were an amiable and delightful couple and their idiosyncrasies were more than offset by their kindliness.

44

All this was fifty years ago, and they have, since many years, been gone. I believe they both went to the same place. The major could surely have beguiled Saint Peter.

There was tragedy too. Some miles up the river lived a family. The children were infrequent playmates of ours. The father, a fine southern gentleman, had recently died. It was whispered that up to the last his wife, much younger and very handsome, had tortured him while he lay helpless in his bed; that she would hold a glass of water just out of his reach when he was burning with thirst. Other horrors were rumored, probably quite untrue. Soon after, she married the good-

45

looking steamboat captain whose name had been coupled with hers.

A friend of mine on a neighboring plantation announced the visit of an uncle from a town on the Indian River.

The uncle had shot a man from his dooryard, for some real, or fancied, insult, and concluded that a short vacation and absence were indicated. He made me a boat. He was an attractive homicide.

One day, when I was shopping with my father in Jacksonville, a stout little man came rushing into the store, dashed behind and under the counter, squealing, "Don't shoot! Don't shoot!" and was pursued by a lanky, bewhiskered individual who paid no attention to this admonition, but emptied his revolver as he ran.

THE PIROGUE (CANOEING, FLORIDA), 1921. Watercolor on paper, 7⅝ × 10³⁄₁₆ inches. Estate stamped lower right

We made the rest of our purchases further up the street!

Each grocery store had its bar. They had them quite openly, without swing doors.

It was before the time of manufactured ice, and it amused me to see butter in liquid form, ladled out to customers.

48

My sister and I frequently went inland, through the pinewoods, to play with Uncle Albert's children. The distance was perhaps two miles, but we made a long and adventurous voyage of it, first through the little woods of scrub oak, chinquapin and gum trees, then through the trackless pine forest (as we preferred to think of it.). We might encounter a gopher—a large land tortoise—whose hole in the sand was usually shared by a great chicken snake. We would meet with little other life, excepting the birds and chameleons. Here and there a Negro would be digging ginseng roots to be shipped to China. Overhead always floated the buzzard.

Usually boys wore no shoes and in the summer one leapt from one patch of grass to another to avoid the burning sand, being always cautious not to land on sand spurs.

following page: HOEING, JACKSONVILLE, 1921. Watercolor on paper, 7½ × 9½ inches. Estate stamped lower right

In the morning before the dew was off the grass, one put on shoes. Otherwise one would surely contract "ground itch" which, I believe, was afterwards proved to be hookworm.

I had ground itch several times. Still, when I feel a disinclination to work, a normal condition with me, I wonder . . .

One morning I slipped on my shoes, which had been left on the porch overnight. A red-hot pain shot through my foot. I screamed and kicked off my shoes. A scorpion had been disturbed in its snug retreat.

The hottest months in summer we spent in Mayport, at the mouth

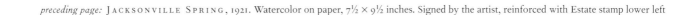

preceding page: JACKSONVILLE SPRING, 1921. Watercolor on paper, 7½ × 9½ inches. Signed by the artist, reinforced with Estate stamp lower left

of the Saint John's river. The trip there was a lovely one, winding

in and out on the small stern-wheeled steamer, stopping at every

landing for no apparent reason unless it were to give the shiftless

crackers some excitement.

One spot was reputed to have been a landing place of Ponce de

Leon, and if he did not find the spring of eternal youth, it was because

he did not look far enough. Surely it is there.

I believe I found it myself once: such a crystal clear pool hidden

deep among the jasmine covered trees, and tangled with grape vines,

in a hammock I had never come across before. I started drinking but spat it out with disgust. It was sulfur water. I must have swallowed some. My hair is still black at sixty.

As we approached the ocean, the river broadened. To the left lay Fort George Island; to the right the little quarantine port of Mayport. Perhaps these are important towns now. Then there were a few houses and a small fleet of pilot boats, and up the beach a barrack of a hotel, something tipped out of plumb by the wind. We had a small cottage, which my uncle's family shared with us. We spent our days bathing and fishing; our nights, slapping mosquitoes.

PULLING IN SHARK, 1921. Watercolor and pencil on paper, 9⅛ × 12⅜ inches. Estate stamped lower left

I recall a friend of my Aunt Fannie, a very stout lady, giving my aunt a lesson in diving from a rowboat.

"Look, Fannie, do it this way," and she put her fat arms upright and fell on the water with a resounding smack. Nothing happened excepting a considerable displacement of the water. And my Aunt Fannie, who was thin, did it that way. We helped her tenderly ashore and after a time she could breathe again.

At low tide, we fished from the jetty. The rocks of which it had been built had been brought from far, as there is not a pebble in that part of Florida.

We fished with hand lines and pulled in anything from hideous toadfish up.

One day I hooked a sea turtle by the flipper. I had a choice of going with him or letting go my hold, so he bore my line away.

In the intervals of fishing we ate oysters cracked from the rocks.

Fort George Island, where the pilot boats lay, was once a rendezvous for pirates. We had several treasure hunts, but the pirates must have been an impoverished lot, or else preferred keeping their treasure in their pockets.

At low tide one day I waded out to a little island on which was an oyster bed. I played about 'till the tide had risen, nearly covering the island. Then the oysters opened their sharp blades and my feet were badly cut before I reached shore.

Razor backed hogs roamed the beach, eating the jellyfish washed up by the tide. We believed they ate small children too. We usually kept together so as to give the hogs a choice. We didn't think they would take more than one at a time, and each trusted it would be a friend. Fortunately, the jellyfish were plentiful.

THE SAINT JOHN'S RIVER, 1921. Watercolor on paper, 7½ × 9½ inches. Estate stamped lower left

The port doctor, when not doing his quarantine duties, would fish for shark from a rowboat. His equipment was a rope the thickness of a clothesline, tied to an enormous hook baited with a mullet. This he would troll from his boat. His Negro helper rowed and when a shark was hooked he was allowed to tow the boat about until worn out, and was then hauled ashore. Perhaps this was not very sporting fishing but there were shark to spare and they did very well to fertilize the orange trees.

We felt badly when the time came to close our cottage and leave for home. It meant winter was approaching and we disliked winter.

Sometimes the weather was so severe that we must put on our
shoes and stockings. It seemed hard to us. Also, we must return to school.

We spent several years in Florida, and then returned to Michigan.

The year after our leaving, there was a scourge of yellow fever in
Jacksonville.

The ferry no longer ran and all communication was cut off from

our side of the river. Only my Uncle Albert, who had a motor boat,
would venture over to the town for supplies and medicines, and only he
would nurse the isolated cases in our neighborhood.

He never, in all his life, found time to provide comforts for himself and his family. The calls on him from the poor whites and the Negroes were too many. His family was cheerful and philosophical about it and admitted that, being himself, he couldn't act otherwise.

There were none but Negro churches in our neighborhood and my uncle read services at his home each Sunday morning, for all who would attend, and nearly all did.

My father was a good man too, but my uncle was a saint.

FISHING FOR STARS, 1921 Watercolor on paper, 7 × 9¾ inches. Private collection

Hollis Taggart Galleries

48 EAST 73 STREET   NEW YORK CITY 10021   TEL 212 628 4000   FAX 212 717 4119

WEB SITE: WWW.HOLLISTAGGART.COM   EMAIL: HOLLISTAGGART@HOLLISTAGGART.COM

MONDAY TO FRIDAY 10 TO 5, SATURDAY 11 TO 5